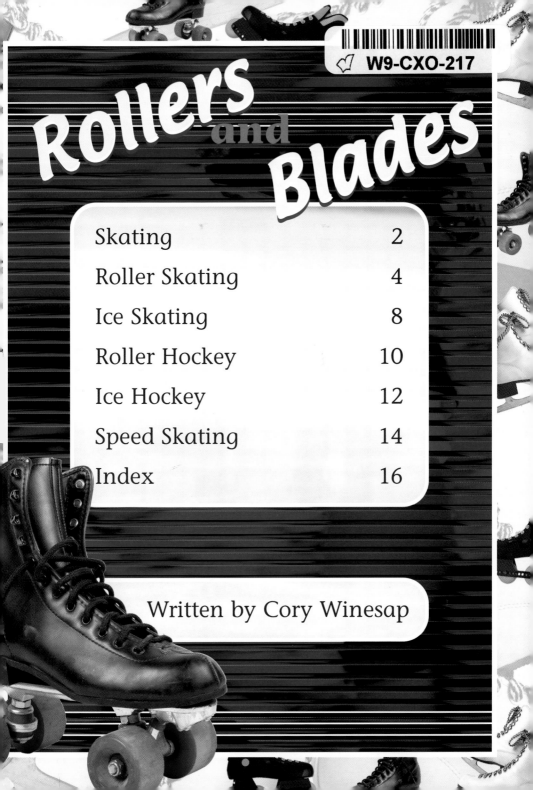

Rollers and Blades

Written by Cory Winesap

Skating

There are two kinds of skating, roller skating and ice skating.

Roller skating

Ice skating

Roller Skating

Roller skates have four wheels.
Some roller skates
have the four wheels in a line.

Types of Roller Skates

four wheels in a line

Some roller skates
have two wheels in front
and two wheels behind.

two wheels behind

two wheels in front

You can roller-skate inside or outside. You can roller-skate inside on rinks.

These people are roller-skating inside.

You can roller-skate outside on hard ground.

These people are roller-skating outside.

Ice Skating

Ice skates have blades.

You can ice-skate inside on rinks.

This girl is ice-skating inside.

You can ice-skate
outside when it is very cold.
You can ice-skate
on frozen ponds or lakes.

This woman is ice-skating outside.

Roller Hockey

You can play hockey
on roller skates.
This kind of hockey
is called roller hockey.

A roller hockey team

There are five players
on a roller hockey team.
One player is the goalkeeper.
The goalkeeper guards the goal.
The other players try to hit the ball
into the goal.

Roller Hockey Goalkeeper

helmet

chest pad

catch glove

stick

blocking pad

leg pad

roller skate

ball

11

Ice Hockey

You can play hockey on ice skates.

This kind of hockey is called ice hockey.

Playing ice hockey

There are six players
in an ice hockey team.
One player is the goalkeeper.
The other players try to hit the puck
into the goal.

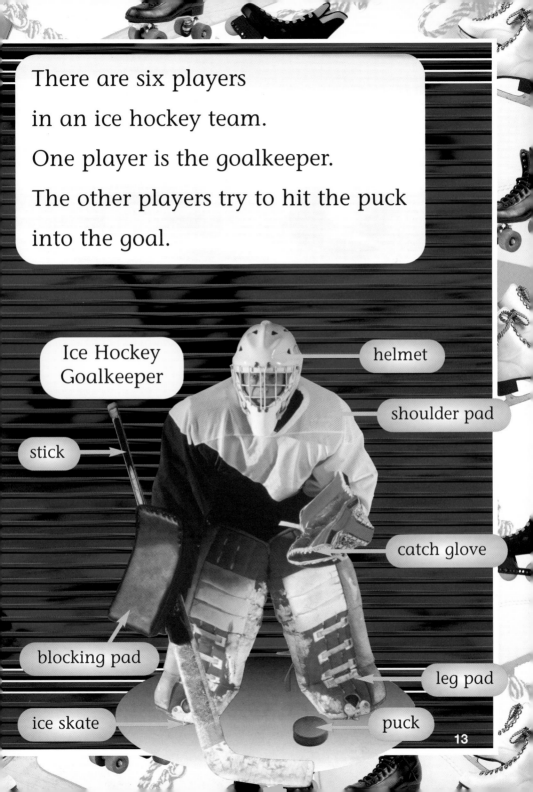

Ice Hockey
Goalkeeper

helmet

shoulder pad

stick

catch glove

blocking pad

leg pad

ice skate

puck

13

Speed Skating

Some people skate very fast on roller skates.
Some people skate very fast on ice skates.

Ice speed skating

Skating very fast is called speed skating. People speed-skate inside and outside.

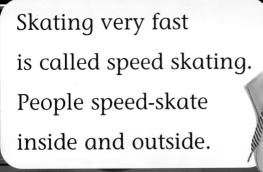

2002 Olympic
Ice Speed Skating Champions

Name	Event	Country
arc Gagnon	500 m	Canada
ng Yang	500 m	China
athieu Turcotte	1000 m	Canada
ng Yang	1000 m	China
ong-Sung Kim	1500 m	Korea
n-Kyung Choi	1500 m	Korea

Index